Praise for
MISCHIEVERSE

Rude, irreverent and downright filthy ... like Johnny Rotten meets Pam Ayres.

Julia Lewis, Actor (*Their Finest*)

This wonderful book gave me many laugh-out-loud moments. So many observations that resonated – the absurdities of modern life. It's great to pick up and open a page when the world seems chaotic, and puts a smile on the face immediately. Brilliantly written!

Jane Hatton, Founder and CEO, evenbreak.co.uk

Snarky, quirky, downright rude, Suze skewers pop culture: its language, fashion, politics, entertainment. Not even family and cherished holidays escape her cutting wit. Through it all, she manages to make us laugh at ourselves and the silliness of contemporary life.

Barbara Grengs, Author of the Toby Martin series of children's mystery novels and *Delicate Dames* (forthcoming)

PMSL at 'Donald the Politician' ... one to sing at Christmas

Sarah Setterfield, Chief Inspiration Officer, weareinspirato.com

An amusing sideways look at anything and everything - I love that it's so wide ranging. The perfect gift for anyone who glories in potty-mouthed poetry!

A. E. Rawson, Author of *A Savage Art*

About
Suzan St Maur

Canadian-born, UK-based Suzan St Maur is a bestselling non-fiction author, international business writer, and founder of the award-winning website resource HowToWriteBetter.net. She also works extensively in the third sector, amongst other things, contributing to charities in cancer survivorship (she has had cancer twice). In addition, she writes joke books, and *Mischieverse* is the latest outlet for her wit, as well as being an excellent way to let off steam.

MISCHIEVERSE

SELECTED WORKS BY THE SAME AUTHOR

Non-fiction

The Jewellery Book (with Norbert Streep)
The Home Safety Book
The A to Z of Video and AV Jargon
Writing Words That Sell (with John Butman)
Powerwriting: the hidden skills you need to transform your business writing
Wedding Speeches for Women
The A to Z of Wedding Wisdom

Humour

The Horse Lover's Joke Book
Canine Capers: over 350 jokes to make your tail wag
The Country Lover's Joke Book
The Pony Lover's Joke Book

MISCHIEVERSE

Rude humour that laughs at life's irritations

or

Poetic reflections on how bloody stupid life can be

Suzan St Maur

CORONA BOOKS

First published in the United Kingdom in 2017
by Corona Books UK
www.coronabooks.com

Copyright © Suzan St Maur, 2017
www.mischieverse.com

The moral right of the author has been asserted.

All rights reserved.

No part of this publication may be reproduced, stored in a retrieval system, or transmitted, in any form or by any means, without the prior permission in writing of the publisher, nor be otherwise circulated in any form of binding or cover other than that in which it is published and without a similar condition including this condition being imposed on the subsequent purchaser.

ISBN 978-0-9932472-8-6

Cover design by Nina Taylor based on an idea by the author.
Title page illustrations by Nina Taylor
Copyright © Nina Taylor, 2017
www.taylormaiddesigns.co.uk

For Jaff
…who tells me off for swearing

Warning: adult humour
(in places, very adult humour)

Contents

Introduction 13

Chapter 1: Daily Life

Measure what? 16
After the guests leave 17
The plug-ged sink 18
'O Root Canal' 20
Knees 22
Bathroom brainfarts 24
Garbage 26
Blister packs 27
'50 Days to Clean Your Oven' 28
Pneumonia 30
Roaring fire 32
Kids 34

Chapter 2: Animals

Horses on the highway 38
Nursery rhymes for horses 39
Nursery rhymes for dogs 41
Shite birds 44
Doggy bags 46
Puddytat 48
Big TC 50

Chapter 3: Food and Fashion

Diets and booze	54
Wine	56
Orange shoes	58
Glamping	60
Fast food	62
On my tit	64
Man buns	66
Caesar salad	68

Chapter 4: Words

Fresh	70
Incontinence	72
Selfies	74
Syllables	76
Iconic	78
Awesome	80
Let's conversate	81
How to write better	82
Smug	84
Yummy	86

Chapter 5: Behaviour

Willy waving	90
21st century swearing	92
International swearing	94
Germans	96
Twerking	98
'Can you hear me?'	100
Body building	102

Chapter 6: Politics and Media

Old Britannia	106
Alternative facts	108
In the Huff Post	110
Absolutely clear	112
'Yankee Doodle' re-written	114
Reality TV	116
POTUS and FLOTUS	118
Bigly	120

Chapter 7: Seasonal

Dry Christmas	122
'Donald the Politician'	123
Post-Christmas poem	124
'Jingle Bills'	126
Daffodils? In January?	127
Fireworks Night	128
Valentine's Day – a poem	130
Valentine's Day – card verses from Hell	131
Valentine's Day – roses are red	132
Valentine's Day – the grammar police	134
Easter beaster	136

Introduction

Whenever life's little irritations and absurdities piss you off, have a browse in this book. In fact, if you get pissed off a lot, you might like to carry it with you at all times.

In it you'll find that I have vented my spleen about many of the things you probably vent your spleen about, and hopefully in a way that will make you laugh. Laughter is, after all, the best antidote to irritation and beats the hell out of pulling the wings off live flies.

So not only is *Mischieverse* therapy for you, but also it will achieve the following for those you care about, when life has got on your tits:

- Your cat will be grateful not to be kicked or shouted at
- Your neighbours will not be offended by your flipping them the bird
- Your fellow motorists will be spared a blast of your horn
- Your partner will not have to stay out until you've gone to bed
- Your kitchen utensils will remain in good, unbroken condition
- Your mobile/cell phone glass will remain uncracked
- Your Facebook friends won't have to comfort you
- You'll be far less likely to get sued for slander

Enjoy. And laugh with me.

Suzan St Maur

Daily Life

MEASURE WHAT?

Measurements are really weird
They come from varied sources
Around the globe the experts state
(Whoever reinforces).

Metric, US, Imperial
Would help if they were standardised
But logic being what logic is
Our choices are just bastardised.

Explain to me if you just can
Why, for example, Canada
Has kilometres for its roads
But ounces for food data?

And take the UK if you will
A 'European' nation
Still travelling on in good old miles
But suffering from frustration …

…when told they cannot sell in pounds
For veg, fruit, fish and roasts
It's kilos only, or that's it
You mention pounds? You're toast.

I really wish someone would think
Of measures international
That let us cook and drink and eat
In ways not so irrational.

AFTER THE GUESTS LEAVE

Well, that was fun, now! Wasn't it just?
Eating and drinking and shooting the breeze
Partying blindly from morning to dusk
Consuming all victuals with casual ease.

When the last of them left over lingering goodbyes
As I looked at my watch and yawned a few times
And the last winter coat was pulled on just akimbo
I flicked the electrics to nix the door chimes.

The first thing I did was to switch off the light
Then stepped out of my elegant Jimmy Choo heels
Which though so snazzy are fiendishly tight
And put my phalanges through awful ordeals.

Next came my belt which though being a Versace
Has to be tight to pull in my abdomen
So when it comes off needs a bloody good scratchee
A slap and a massage with fingers a-roamin'.

Now comes the best part most easily, by far
With a ping and a pop and a flip and a flop
It is that moment when off comes my bra
Not all that smart, but now it's off I can't stop.

Down come the tights, or the pantyhose even
Depending on whether you're Brit or a Yankee
By this stage I don't care if I look uneven
It's late and I'm tired, boy – no hanky panky.

At last it is bedtime and as I just mentioned
I feel as sexy as a muddy drain cover
So don't count on me for romantic intentions
But there's always tomorrow when we're fresh and recovered.

THE PLUG-GED SINK

Oh, curs-ed spite*, we're in the shite
The kitchen sink is plug-ged
That greasy pan whose yuk just swam
Right down the drain? It's buggered.

That's all we need, indeed, indeed
When guests are due for dinner
How can I drain the leaves romaine
And use my salad spinner?

I know, I know, it's not as though
This issue is life threatening
But bloody hell, it's just as well
Our guests are so unquestioning.

What can I do, when wading through
Grease water to my elbows
While trying to serve the chilled hors d'oeuvres
With hands like a dirty hobo's?

OK, let's try to be a bit sly
And use that suction pumper
Guess what? It failed and promptly baled
Six gallons up my jumper.

Right: now's the time to beat the grime
And take this bastard seriously
Pour caustic soda down its throat
And blast its balls just viciously.

Yee hah! Guess what? We kicked its butt
At last we'll get the food we love
But wait a tick, I forgot to flick
The 'on' switch on our kitchen stove.

Sorry folks, it's time to coax
Our nearest barbecue guru
Get grilling now and cook somehow
While I search out a corkscrew.

Here, have some wine; it's mighty fine
And looks a damned sight tastier
Than the filthy drink that was in my sink
Plus pouring it's much easier.

*From *Omelette* by William Shakespeare.

'O ROOT CANAL'
(to be sung to the tune of 'O Christmas Tree')

O Root Canal! O Root Canal!
I'm up for this procedure
O Root Canal! O Root Canal!
Tomorrow, this sheer torture
I'd rather stick a dragonfly
Right in the centre of my eye
O Root Canal! O Root Canal!
I'm think I'm due a seizure.

O Root Canal! O Root Canal!
No sleep had I last evening
O Root Canal! O Root Canal!
My husband says he's leaving
All I could say the whole night long
Was tie a knot in his poor dong
O Root Canal! O Root Canal!
My heart and breast are heaving.

O Root Canal! O Root Canal!
My dentist is awaiting
O Root Canal! O Root Canal!
My terror not abating
I'll need more time, as after all
I'm clinging halfway up his wall
O Root Canal! O Root Canal
I need some kind placating.

O Root Canal! O Root Canal!
I'm in the chair, strapped tightly
O Root Canal! O Root Canal!
I'm sat here quite contritely
After he stuck me in the arm
With something called diazeparm
O Root Canal! O Root Canal!
I look upon you brightly.

KNEES

I must be getting old, I think
And modern clothes are a mystery
Some new trends to me just stink
Of sheer, unfathomed lunacy.

Like, for instance, chop a slit
In your trousers half way down
So your knees burst through a split
And protrude like an uncooked prawn.

Why, oh why, do we need to see
Your scabby, shabby knobbly joints
Let's face it, it's a bony knee
That sticks through jeans at a crucial point.

Then there's more than knees and fashions
Ripped new pants and tears away
Especially if you love Kardashians
Sticking knees through Versace.

Maybe I'm just old and boring
But when I buy some jeans or jacket
Having paid designer fortunes
Cut them up? You're kidding! F**k it.

Yes, my knees may be decrepit
Having lived long past my teens
But I'm buggered if I'll slice it
Through the knees of designer jeans.

Let's be honest: knees can't do
Things to make them sexy, cute?
Maybe tarted up and showing through?
Knees don't work if you're astute.

Even if you're a keen Kardashian
In my view, keep scissors away
By all means buy pants in fashion
But keep them whole for another day.

BATHROOM BRAINFARTS

Strange how high emotions run
In family bathrooms everywhere
It's high stress plumbing time, not fun
In haste and pulled-on underwear.

Homes with countless bathrooms win
By nixing painful line-ups
A peaceful pee, so tranquilly
But does that negate f**k-ups?

I don't think so, and here's why
Stress reaches out much farther
When time is short, folks tend to snort
And bitch about each other.

There's nothing worse when time is tight
Than getting through your poopy
Then finding that the toilet roll
Has come to the end of its loopy.

A message to all bathroom users
Should be stuck up by the taps:
If the toilet roll has run out
You run out before you craps…

…find another toilet roll first
Then resume your dumping stance
Accomplish your bowel motions
In a not-guilty circumstance.

Then of course we get the toothpaste
Twats who strangle it so dry
Leave the top off, splash it down
Piss off others so, by and by.

Clue: it's simple, just remember
Toothpaste isn't free for all
Go buy your own f**king toothpaste
And observe its protocol.

Next the age-old argument
The seat: is up, or down now?
In a multi-gender household
This can raise an eyebrow.

It can also raise some hell
Akin to World War Threesome
So I would advise you all
To try to do 'agree some'.

And whatever bathroom bitches
Out over which you folks might fall
Remember things so scatological
Are just piss and shit – that's all.

GARBAGE

Political correctness now spreads right into the rubbish
(Or garbage if you live towards the west of the Atlantic)
So much as we continue to throw out the normal bullshit
We're leaned upon to file our crap in detail that's just frantic.

Here I speak from experience of life in Western nations
Where sorting out your garbage ranges from a bit to ludicrous
OK, it's fair to sort stuff to avoid those junk mutations
But colours, sizes, fabrics, hues – to me it's just ridiculous.

Let's take bottles, empty ones, to serve us for a start
It's not enough that they're made of glass: no, glass has many shades
We have to line them up in hues as finely drawn as art
So garbage folks can throw them in the rightly coloured grades.

Then of course there's garden waste, from weeds to short grass cuttings
How do we group the browns and greens, in classifiable clippings?
And God forbid the spade should skid and dogshit's in the gubbins
No, garden waste must make post-haste for purely PC pickings.

Next on the list is metal stuff from tin cans to aluminum
(Or aluminium if you're British and a Grammar Nazi)
Metallurgists, you're right at home; but for us it's pandemonium
Meanwhile it's harder to get right than languages like Swazi.

And d'you know what? Here's where my nasty sneaky little brain
Departs from PC thoughts and just starts festering
Suspecting now that all this stuff as garbage or recycling
All gets dumped in landfill sites – the same ones: sweet sequestering.

BLISTER PACKS

Blister packs, heady whacks
Why are these so fiddly?
Break your nails, right off the rails
And all you get is diddly?...

...maybe just a pill to pop
But if your nails are treasures
Trust me, blister packs will f**k
All manicures and pleasures.

When such packs are properly made
Their aluminium's toughest
Which when you try to get the pill
Will challenge muscles roughest.

Ah, but now that costs are cut
Such blister packs get shrivelled
Their balls cut off, and wafer thin
So all substance is repelled.

Makes it easier for people
Who like me value our nails
But what happens when we press out
Tablets from such wanky fails?

Sure the tabs drop nice and easy
In your hand if you're alert
But you can swallow aluminium
Crap along with meds inert.

Trust me, blister packs can fool you
Never shove their stuff up yours
Check their metal covers haven't
F**ked up your digestive powers.

50 DAYS TO CLEAN YOUR OVEN

Are you old enough to remember that wonderful Paul Simon song '50 Ways to Leave Your Lover'? Here's my version of the lyrics for you to sing along with.

A filthy oven is disgusting that's for sure
Especially when your kitchen's otherwise so pure
It's just a bugger, a cleaning job we must endure
Each 50 days, you clean your oven.

Such grease and stinky crap and baked-on rotten food
It's all you need to put you in a filthy mood
But roll your sleeves up, don't be such a f**king prude
Each 50 days, you clean your oven.
Fifty days to clean your oven.

Get out the hose, Rose
Prepare the bin, Lynn
Take off the trash, Ash
Just get down and scrub
Work with some spray, Ray
Use that elbow grease, Reece
Scour it to death, Beth
Go rub-a-dub-dub.

(repeat chorus)

Just when you've got that sludge across your kitchen floor
That's when a bell will ring – there's someone at the door
Tell them to f**k off: you don't need them any more
You need 50 ways to clear the mess up.

At last the oven's finished and looks all pristine
You're bathed in shit and not a sight that should be seen
Cheer up kiddo, there's seven weeks there in between
Now and next time oven's dirty…

Get out the hose, Rose
Prepare the bin, Lynn
Take off the trash, Ash
Just get down and scrub
Work with some spray, Ray
Use that elbow grease, Reece
Scour it to death, Beth
Go rub-a-dub-dub.

(repeat chorus)

PNEUMONIA

Bugger you, I've got the flu
No wait – it's now pneumonia.
I know I'm right, saw the blue light
And heard that loud sironia.

Nurses, doctors, helicopters
With tubes and masks and cannulas
Bit of a fright? Too f**king right.
Strapping me down like an animal.

'Hallucinating, that she is,'
So said some passing flunkies
'They often do, with pneumandoo
Just rant and rave, like junkies.'

'What's wrong with all these stupid dicks?'
I snarled at my son, who was cowering
'Lazy, stupid little pricks
Can't they see we should all be showering?'

'My mum's delirious,' smiled my son
'This rudeness isn't typical'
'We've got to get this job tonight'
I screamed at no one in particular.

And so it went, the embarrassment
Me shouting like a euphonium
For five whole days and nights ablaze
Thanks to that bug, pneumonium.

Several times I'm told I said
The staff were f**king morons
And just precisely where to stick
Their pills and jabs and so-on.

Familiar nightmare, so they say
And clinical staff are used to it
But I wonder just how many of them
Have actually been through it?

You feel your brain has been hit by a train
That it's fallen down a gully
You can see real life but it's out of reach
Much though you push and pully.

So thanks, pneumonia, for the chance
To chase after my own sanity
It's made me think that staying sane
Is much more than just vanity.

ROARING FIRE

Oh, I love a roaring fire
Such a welcome sight to see
Glowing in our living room
Inspires peace so lovingly.

Dogs and cats and children so
…love to huddle up that close
Toasting little faces there
A warming experience for most.

When a whoopsie should occur
Log drops down and sets fire
…to the rug we love so much
Never mind! That's not so dire.

Quickly get a water jug
To stop the flames from burning hell
Someone, quick, just piss right there
It may smell foul, but works as well.

Next day once the fire's gone out
And the folks have f**ked off too
Daylight shows shit everywhere
Ashes, dust and crap askew.

Call upon the family now
You love your roaring fire so much
So it's time to clean the mess
Takes more than just a gentle touch.

Ashes, dust and dirt so manky
Left for Mum or Dad at home
What a task so grim and wanky
Foul parental work syndrome.

Next time spread it 'cross the family
Want a fire? OK, right…
Stack it up and light it then
Next day YOU clean up the shite.

Think I'm being unromantic?
Maybe, but who gives a f**k?
Roaring fires, in honest truth are
…a few hours' joy, plus endless muck.

KIDS

Don't these assholes drive you nuts?
What happened to those tots so cute?
Grow away, leave you behind
Yet when in shit, back home they scoot?

Love them dearly, wipe their bums
Cherish them and all their friends
Clean up the puke, beer, pizza fumes
Comfort them when the party ends…

Deal with all those teenage angsts
Hormones raging, putrid zits
Dramas, fights and slamming doors
Turns them into little shits.

Whatever happened to my sweet
…little son or daughter then?
Just what turned them into such
…a growling monster, alien?

Then one day, the fog just clears
They ask you if you feel OK
And suddenly you're not, because
You're gob-smacked that they asked that way.

Now when things are smoothing out
Your brat is human, finally
Off they go in search of freedom
And you're left, bereft, empty.

Never mind, that's what we're here for
Parents are a f**king bore
Just around to pay their bills then
…'bugger off' no need, no more.

So, don't these assholes drive you nuts?
What happened to those tots so cute?
Grow away, leave you behind
Yet when in shit, back home they scoot?

Tell you something, 'tween us both
Being here for them is joyful
When they get in shite, no matter
…what, we're always loyal.

Much as kids may assholes be
We parents are restricted
…'cause when those grandkids come along
We soon become addicted.

Animals

HORSES ON THE HIGHWAY

Some motorists are very kind
To horses somewhat heated
You slow and stop, with engines off,
So we can remain seated.

The trouble is once we have gone
Beyond your line of vision
You goose your engine, roaring loud
With racing-start precision.

Creating thus some equine fear
Your clutch engages, wallop!
Your tyres bite on earth and shit
Then horse goes into gallop.

And lorry drivers, you're the best
At seeing us fast departed.
If when we're feet from a lorry's rear
Your airbrakes have just farted.

So though we're grateful for the thought
From all you careful drivers
Please wait till we're truly past
Or you'll need to revive us.

NURSERY RHYMES FOR HORSES

Hickory dickory dock
Jump off against the clock
The horse struck one
Four faults were done
'Oh, Hickory dickory … f**k!'

Ring a ring a rosies
Is where my pony's nose is
A-tishoo, a-tishoo
That'll teach him to nibble at hedges out on a hack.

Little Miss Maddle sat in the saddle
Eating her Burger King
When came a bike rider that revved up beside her
And her horse began fast galloping
Poor Little Miss Maddle fell out of the saddle
Straight onto her safety hat
Still clutching her burger her shouts threatened murder
'Now I can't have my french fries with that!'

Jack and Jill went up the hill
To try to jump the water
Jack made a hash and fell with a splash
But Jill jumped clear as one oughta.

Mary had a little horse
Which kicked like there's no tomorrow
And everywhere that Mary went
No other horse dared follow

Three stroppy mares
Three stroppy mares
See how they bite
See how they bite
They all ran after the farrier
And bit him on his posterior
It made him feel so inferior, three stroppy mares

Mary Mary quite contrary
How did the dressage test go?
Counter-canter went well but my half-pass was hell
So in all it was quite a poor show.

Little Bo-Porse got bucked off her horse
And she's no idea where to find him
Leave him alone, he'll make his way home
Trailing his reins behind him

Oats, chaff, maize and sugar beet go
Oats, chaff, maize and sugar beet go
Can you or I or anyone know
How that pony keeps raiding the feed bins, ho-ho?

Little Boy Blue, don't blow your horn
My horse is so fizzy
He's being fed on corn
What would occur if you blew it, d'you think?
We'd be in the next county before you could blink.

Neigh, neigh, racehorse
Have you got a brain?
No sir, no sir
Just a fancy name.
I spook at the master

I spook at the dame
I spook at nearly everything I see down the lane.

Old MacDonald had a yard
Ee-i-ee-i-oh
And on that yard he had some livery owners
Ee-i-ee-i-oh
With a gossip-gossip here
And a gossip-gossip there
Scandal, intrigue everywhere
Old MacDonald had a yard
Ee-i-ee-i-oh

NURSERY RHYMES FOR DOGS

Hickory dickory dock
A Collie watched his flock
A bee stung his nose
So hard that he froze
And stood still while his flock ran amok.

Ring a ring a rosies
Is where my puppy's nose is
A-tishoo, a-tishoo
He's just discovered the hard way that roses have thorns.

Little Miss Whippet
Was no more than a snippet
Sniffing the curds and whey
When along came a spider
Started eating beside her
'I'll teach him,' she thought, 'right away.'
So little Miss Whippet
Despite being a snippet

Stood up and started to squeal
The spider was shock-ed
Took off like a rocket
And Miss Whippet partook of the meal.

Jack and Jill went up the hill
To fetch their dog some water
But when they returned the dog was concerned
With guzzling their nice bread and bawt-ter.

Mary had a little pup
Its teeth were sharp as razors
And everywhere that Mary went
It tore things up to blazes.

Three Setter dogs
Three Setter dogs
See how they run
See how they run
The owner's jumping up and down
And shouting like a demented clown
But the Setters are off for a night on the town
Three Setter dogs

Mary Mary quite contrary
How was obedience class?
Sit and stay went quite well but our 'walkies' were hell
'Specially when I fell on my ass.

Little Bo-Peep has lost her sheep
And she's no idea where to find them
The sheepdog pulled a stunt with a nice bitch's c**t
Flipped the bird and left her to mind them.

Oats, peas, beans and barley go
Oats, peas, beans and barley go
Can you or I or anyone know
What sort of dogfood is that, by Jove?

Little Kerry Blue, don't blow your horn
Or growl or snarl
When my trousers you've torn
Or bark when you see me come down to your house
After all, I'm a postman - I'm a man, not a mouse

Neigh, neigh, Poodle
Have you got a brain?
No sir, no sir
Just a fancy name.
I bark at the master
I bark at the dame
I bark at every f**king thing I see down the lane.

Old MacDonald had a kennel
Ee-i-ee-i-oh
And in that kennel he had 20 dogs
Ee-i-ee-i-oh
With a woof-woof here
And a growl-growl there
Someone let the cat in, chaos everywhere
Old MacDonald had a kennel
Ee-i-ee-i-oh

SHITE BIRDS

How I love the birds who go shit
On my windshield and what's more
All over my back yard – and yet it
Matters not. I love them all.

Those feathery little bastards who do
Sit on my fence before the feeder
Crap on the wood with acidic poo-poo
Playing food-follow-my-leader.

Looking out of my office window
I can see those birds line up
Like the aircraft there in limbo
Coming into land abrupt.

What is it that makes these shite birds
Heed their air traffic control?
I would love to know the code words
That they use for flight patrol.

In the meantime shite is gathering
On the rotting wooden bits
Of the fence that takes a hammering
Where the birdies craps and sits.

What to do, oh birdie lovers?
Tell my cats to kill them now?
Sit here shouting at their mothers
Get them out and fast – and how?

Nah. It's simple when you think it
Move the f**king feeders – yeah
Right away from all that junk it's
Up the garden somewhere far.

Now the feeders are in placement
Up the back yard, bird shite-free
But I'm looking from the basement
So it's hard to hear or see.

Never mind folks, shite birds know us
Right inside our hearts they dwell
Never forget to share your focus
On those little shits we love so well.

DOGGY BAGS

Does your dog go shit outside
Way beyond your garden?
Has he shat but you have lied
And not cleared up after him?

Naughty you, not PC too
A slap for doggie's mum/dad
OK, let's not step in dogs' shite
But really, it's not that bad.

What the worthies twitch about
Are worms and bugs transmissible
If kiddies pick and eat dog shit
But surely, not permissible?

Makes me smile when thinking on
How dog shit's so pernicious
When bacteria in your mouth
Are many times more vicious.

Dog shit, so undoubtedly
Is f**king foul to step in
Smelly, gross, disgustingly
A nightmare, sure, to tread in.

But before we slag off dogs
Condemn them as pure vermin
Let's stop to think why they're with us
Their purpose now, determine.

Dogs are friends like nothing else
As pals, companions, soul mates
So if they shit now, what the hell
What really matters, these dates?

Owning dogs is now PC
Provided that they're bijou
So if they shit it has to be
In plastic bag so (non-U).

Do you really, really like
Such little dogs so fancy?
That can crap into a bag
With accuracy chancy?

Dogs, to me, are proper beasts
Not apologies for canines
And because I love them so
I'll scoop their anal foul lines.

PUDDYTAT

Puddytat, I love you so, but your arrogance is stifling
When you yowl to get outside and force me to obey
You sit there, bored and yawing wide, your interest merely trifling
'I may go out, but maybe not. There's time to spare till doomsday.'

Much as I respect my cats I do get twitchy waiting
For them to make decisions as to if it's in or out
For f**k's sake make your mind up, you small creature so dictating
I'm freezing here while you just cogitate your f**king doubt.

Yes, it's raining. Sorry, puss. There's nothing to be done for it
I can't control the weather or world politics or more
We mere humans aren't like you: we're made to follow rules and shit
So be a good dear puddytat, get off your ass, f**k off out the door.

'Hmmm, I've changed my mind, OK? I think I'll have some dinner now
Though it's only lunchtime surely there's a lot more salmon?'
You little scrounging asshole, you know that there's lots more anyhow
Do you care that food like this could help us beat world famine?

Er, where are you, puddytat? Thought I saw you disappearing now
Never heard you leaving our backdoor step, must admit
Given we were having a good talk about things so highbrow
Am hoping you're still there to comment well upon this shit.

Puddytat, er, puddytat – I'm waiting for some sense from you
But, er, where the f**k are you now, you sneaky little gobshite?
Ah well, I will simply go to bed and hope we hear a little 'mew'
And guess what? You are right there, a fat lump on my bed site.

Now move over, puddytat. Much as some may question it
This is my bed. It says here: 'a king-size for two occupants'
Seeing that four dogs are here plus your feline opposites
Time to rearrange your thoughts 'cause you don't wear the 'cat pants'.

Now we slide into slow sleep, recharging our f**ked batteries
When you turn up and yowl because you caught food for the nest
Tell you what now, puddytat, I'm speed dialling the catteries
Thanks to you we never get a decent night-time's rest.

F**k you, puddytat. Oh OK, you can settle on my duvet (MUST you?)
Hope you don't puke up that mouse on these pristine bed clothes
And in case you're wondering just today they're clean, brand new…
Oh, so sorry now to wake you. Get back to your dreamy doze…

BIG T.C.

Once upon a time there was
A cat called Big TC
(That stood for 'Tiger Cat' of course)
A brutal puss, was he.

TC came from friends in Kent
Whose pussy had been ravaged
By the local farmer's tom
Known well to f**k and savage.

TC became mine one day
When having clean forgotten
After a boozy party night
I felt so sick and rotten…

'A kitten? Oh of course I will,'
I blurted out so drunken
Six weeks later email shows
My promise having slunk in.

Little TC wasn't frail
When shown a box for travelling
For the journey back to mine
We had to use wire netting.

And not just netting delicate
But strong enough for elephants
This little bastard was so strong
We couldn't even take a chance.

Wooden crate with borders hard
Netting nailed securely
Stopped TC from climbing t'ward
Beyond my car, so surely.

A great big bully, he became
The terror of the neighbourhood
No other cats could be the same
'Cos he was top cat, understood.

Then one sunny springtime day
When baby birds were blossoming
TC found a nest out front
And climbed right to it, wobbling.

What TC had failed to see
Was Mama blackbird's nest span
Once TC was up the tree
'Twas curtains for his best plan.

In fact not only did he goof
But Mama blackbird f**ked him
Chased him out at highest speed
And scared his pants off, *pro tem*.

Yes, was she successful there
A birdie after blood now
Stormed him out of her small tree
Right up the driveway – pow, pow!

And not just up the driveway but
A follow-up so evil
She pecked his head as he jumped the gate
Which caused him much upheaval.

Dear old TC lived 20 years
And was loved by many
But he never, never tried
To raid birds' nests again-y.

DIETS AND BOOZE

Let's get it straight before starting
I'm overweight by miles
I weigh myself each time, farting
And if an ounce is gone, it's smiles.

Don't do sugar, 'cos the quack
Said diabetes could come soon
If on food I don't cut back
Or booze or other stuff in tune.

Modern diets are all fine and feisty
…dandy although nothing's new
I've got books going back to the 50s
Talking of low carbs that do.

My old dad had one that worked then
Called it 'Drinking Man's Diet'
Simply meant you could drink booze when
Carbs were stripped down on the quiet.

In a word, it meant no sugar
Or no starchy, bloaty shite
Green veg, meat, fish and booze vulgar
But protein, alcohol – alright.

Seems amazing when you think it
That diet was what Air Forces used
In WW2 to keep their pilots
Slim enough to seem unboozed.

Now of course our diets flourish
On the basis of no booze
Booze in no way can us nourish
Other than to make us lose.

Ah, well, now, I must ask it
Is sobriety worthwhile?
Is modern life just pure shit?
Should we accept life so vile?

Here I should turn this poem
Into verse with morals good
But let's get down and f**k 'em
Diet experts made of wood.

Now, what's the answer really
To this question serious
More diets touchy-feely
Even more mysterious?

Nah, just forget that bullshit
Get a grip on fitness real
Use your common sense to work it
Make it what you really feel.

And what happens if you don't do…
…what the fitness gurus say?
'Goodness me, you're in the doo-doo
Unless you do it our way.'

Well, I think it's utter bollocks
To be led so by the nose
Make your own decisions, 'pallocks'
(Yes, that's 'pals' for those who knows!)

WINE

Nothing like a glass of wine
After work, you're home and dry
Pour your stress right down the line
Well – down your throat, to pacify…

…but trouble is, does it really
Make you feel calm and bright?
Or does it blind your hormones
Into thinking all is right?

Flatters hell out of your ego
After glasses, quite a few
'Hey, there's nothing I can't do!'
(Speaks that wine before you spew.)

Someone in my distant past said
Mention something – Latin quote?
They could hit nails on the head
So here is what those Romans wrote.

'In vino veritas,' they stated
When you're pissed you tell the truth
Rude, maybe, and it's fated
To make us all look so uncouth.

Trouble is as we get older
Wine just makes us seem absurd
Youngster pissed on cheap wine – bolder?
Funny – not like us old turds.

In the meantime let's explore those
Literary classics known
Celebrating help for good prose
That we've come to call our own.

Ernest Hemingway put over
Thoughts that booze could pave the way
Said 'write pissed but edit sober'
So, so true. It saves the day.

In the meantime let's just love those
Grapes that make our wine so lush
Red or white or rosé close…
…off our minds to daily mush.

And compared with all that's out there
Pain and politics so vile
Wine deletes our pain points, so where
It can help, it does in style.

ORANGE SHOES

Such nice young men who seem to choose
Alluring jackets, suits and trews
But feet just shod in shocking shoes
Bright orange brogues, no matter whose.

In this good year, Twenty Sixteen
It's hard to know why they're so keen
To shock the eyes of all who've seen
Bright orange brogues, so painfully clean.

Suited now in browns or blues
With shirts and ties a Lord would choose
Matched with belts (and a few tattoos)
They mess it all up with those orange shoes.

Brogues, they're lace-ups, Italian cow hide
Costing more than a private jet ride
Pinching in-grown toenails wild
Making feet feel fashionably deep-fried.

I must share just what I think
Orange brogue shoes frankly stink
Not of feet that sweat or shrink
Just because they're out of sync.

Not sure where you got this notion
That these shoes were such high fashion
Is what you need to get in motion
This awful orange locomotion?

Orange brogues could well look swanky
In an advert from the Yankees
But remember you'll look lanky
And, in tight shoes, will feel cranky.

Do us all a favour, please dear
Dump those orange horrors out there
Give them to a nerd with no care
For fashion. Make them disappear!

GLAMPING

Camping seems bizarre to me
Why sleep so rough when also
Your dear own bed so comfortably
Lets you snore away so?

But weirdos love to play away
And doze on others' manors
And sleep in spots of disarray
Like lying on twenty spanners.

Oh Joy! Here comes the camping style
Where every comfort matters
Where yurts are just so, so worthwhile
To camp in without tatters.

Of course we're just not talking here
Of camping pure and simply
It's 'glamping' in our modern ear
Avoids the plain and pimply.

So what's a yurt, without the hurt?
A tepee from Mongolians
A nice domain to take the pain
From sleeping in Freezolians.

But now in western climes like ours
Our dear old tents don't matters
Without a yurt, not worth a spurt
Or anything else that flatters.

Well, here we go a-glamping now
In yurts or tents or trailers
Luxurious sleeping, yippee, wow!
That's bullshit: mega failures.

Give me my cosy, comfy bed
And yurt inside my homestead
A warm, dry room for me instead
Underneath a homespun bedspread.

FAST FOOD

Here is the latest in fancy fast food
A menu designed to inspire
Us all who would dine if we could find the time
But can only eat food on the flier.

So where do we choose when there's no time to lose?
Yellow arches and names hinting Scottish?
A McShiteBurger's right if you're pushed on the night
But beware: that there *Mc*'s Northern Irish.

Now how 'bout some chicken that's smothered in puke
With spices that castrate your tonsils
And fill your gall bladder with muck even badder
Smoothed on with bug-ridden utensils?

Talking of chicken, Kentucky's the place
Where thousands of foodies get fatter
Colonel Sanders began this digestible scam
No doubt Dunkin' his Donuts in batter.

North of the border it's Canada, eh?
Tim Horton serves coffee ad nauseam
And the Frenchies chime in with disgusting Poutine
All wrapped up in a Beaver Tail scrotum.

In old England the coffee made sewage smell nice
Until someone said, 'It's not wearable!'
Now there's Costa and Starbucks plus copy snackbarf**ks
Serving coffee that's just about bearable.

Meanwhile the fast foodies are getting their kicks
With the brands down and dirty and mean
Burger King's screwing Wendy's, Steak 'n' Shaking her undies
And Hungry Jack wants to shag Dairy Queen.

You've got Domino's Pizza chasing Buffalo Wings
While young Nando just rings Taco's Bell
Krispy Kreme starts a-flowing; the Little Chef's glowing
Wimpy's virtue has gone straight to hell.

After the junk and you've still got some room
If your teeth are decidedly sugary
Timmie's donuts and bits will sweeten your zits
While your blood sugar's all shot to buggery.

So next time you're out feeling feckishly peckish,
Think of this crap that goes on
Still want to savour those revolting flavours?
Shut your eyes, hold your nose, and be strong.

ON MY TIT

First of all, I put my hands up
Speaking plurally don't fit
That's because in life's boobs line-up
I have only one prize tit.

Never mind, such things can get on
One tit just as much as two
Even more so, putting bets on
One sole boob? Packs power, too.

Now for what gets on it these days
Let's explore what really fits
Shitty stuff we sneer at always
That's what gets on most folks' tits.

Let's not go the route of politics
Why? They're mostly stupid twats
Whose views are just audacious tricks
Designed for peasants' habitats.

If you've got a brain that sits
Somewhere above the low IQ
You'll find so much gets on your tits
You'd rather yabbadabbadoo.

Television's a great fit
For stuff that makes you scratch your brain
Pissing off not just your tit
But driving you and yours insane.

TV networks have no money
So produce Kardashians
Reality that's dull, not funny
Unless you love seeing tits askance.

Being a tit I find such bijou
Porn and drama all mixed up
Makes me cringe and want to cut through
All that makes me, well, throw up.

OK, what is lurking out there
That does NOT offend my tit?
How 'bout stories that share elsewhere
Other than tits and bums and shit?

No way can I moralise here
I'm no saint or righteous chief
But my tit would prob'ly endear
Me to solving people's grief.

Bottom line? Get off my tit, folks
If you're pushing utter crap
You know me, I love all those jokes
But my tit knows just what's up.

Get on my tit if you dare to
It will know if you're bullshitting
Hang with me if you want to swear to
Honest crap unremitting.

MAN BUNS

Man buns make my skin just crawl
Such f**king stupid thinking
What do they hope to share withal
And all such crap so stinking?

Like a carbuncle on their crowns
These stupid mounds are growing
Tight elastics causing frowns
Their blood supply not flowing.

In the greater light of things
And future asking questions
What will they do for further flings
When buns outgrow small sessions?

As hair does grow you always know
That buns grow into birds' nests
Of filthy hair that's too long there
So just what's in such manifests?

Here's what I think goes into
Apple-shaped hair buns like this
Nits and gnats and bugs akimbo
Tied up like a Kardashian's tits.

After time of course we wonder
Do those diddy buns reveal
Anything but stinks asunder
After days of dirty hell?

Well, I'd love to see what happens
When I snip the elastic band
Find out what disgusting atoms
Such a bun can keep in hand.

Does it really have to be there
Perched on some fat dickhead's brain?
Does it make him much more likely
To connect with people sane?

No, my thoughts range round to humour
Once again as you expect
Man buns are like a social tumour
At least, that's what I suspect

And when my thoughts turn round to sexy
Could I shag a bunned-up Brit?
I wouldn't risk such apoplexy.
I would rather eat fresh shit.

CAESAR SALAD

Caesar Salad, that's my joy – a culinary homily
Repeated in Brit gastropubs with regular monotony
And Stateside served in volumes big enough to feed a family
But, for me, it's an excuse for sheer and utter gluttony.

Now, God help the commis chef who forgets about anchovies
And not those wanky pseudo fresh jobs, thank you very mucho
I love the salty, bitey, slinky ones that schlepp right up my nosies
To tell the truth I eat them from the can, so there. It's just my
    common toucho.

And then the lettuce which should be a Romaine family member
Although in many restos you'd be so hard-pushed to find that
With luck your lettuce will be classed on indeterminate gender
But never mind – it's always delicieux, no matter what-what.

Next we come to big decisions: chicken bits to amplify?
Not sure those are worth the extra. Depends much on what you
    like
Is it just a tasty salad that your taste buds can't deny?
Or is it an excuse they use to give the price a hike?

Of course, you can have bacon bits within your Caesar special
Or bits of ham or salmon or f**k knows what other such like
But for me, with anchovies, it's perfect: that's official
And shove that other stuff just where the sun don't shine so
    much like.

Here's some advice to restaurateurs who feature Caesar Salads
Don't dick around with their delights: they're brilliant as they
    stand there
Just keep it coming pure and straight with no folkloric ballads
And with anchovies out straight from cans so salty and to die
    fere…

Words

FRESH

Isn't 'fresh' a lovely word?
Invigorates your faith in life
Spices up those sounds unheard
Chases out the cobwebs rife.

Fresh means spring warmth in the air
Singing in the bath or shower
Putting on shades to stop the glare
Of summer sun's impending power.

Fresh is the nip of hunger when
You gaze at fruit and veg before you
Forgetting crappy pesticides, then
Buying twice as much as will do.

Fresh is the cool wind in your hair
Driving your soft-top through the town
Forgetting you're in England where
Five minutes on, rain's pissing down.

Fresh is the thrill of summer clothes
Worn without more woolly layers
Or given that there's nothing froze
Also worn without underwears.

Fresh is what your lover calls you
When you tap them on the shoulder
A gleam in your eye, some innuendo
A grope, a kiss, a little bolder.

Fresh is just the kind of word
To convince you, you can do
Anything, even polish a turd
Or talk your partner into a screw.

Yes, fresh is such a lovely word
Brings new hope and truth inside
Your mind, when life is so absurd
You simply sit on your backside.

INCONTINENCE

Incontinence, incontinence
An ailment oh so widespread
And not just when those older men
Are lying on a deathbed.

Nay, wee-wee worries start from birth
When diapers used as covers
(Or nappies, say the Brits) henceforth
Stop dripping laps for mothers.

As we grow older, year by year
We're never far from pissing
Metaphorical, of course
If drunk, annoyed or missing.

Then 'micturition' lifts its head
It's medics' terminology
Why can't they see it's just plain pee
For a function simply bodily.

But 'micturate' it still remains
And when you come to think of it,
It's not a bad alternative
To words a lot more down to it.

Telling someone to 'micturate off'
Is much, much less insulting
'Micturated' feels much more genteel
Than 'pissed' might be resulting.

All this assumes, of course, that we
Can hold our pee inside us
It's when the flow begins to grow
Out of control – that tries us.

Ladies after giving birth
Sometimes have liquid laughter
Hence the expression 'pissing yourself'
Real consequences after.

For them we have some dainty things
To wear within their underwear
Cute little pads armed with small wads
To reinforce their thunderwear.

And then we have the older men
Whose bladders are just weakening
A tiny bit where e'er they sit
Making bathroom runs a-streakening.

Would we be right were we to say
We're well obsessed with pissing?
Our bodies' needs: such basic deeds
Like sleeping, eating, kissing?

Who knows, but let's remember now
A famous book with branding:
The Yellow Stream, surrealist dream
By author I. P. Standing.

SELFIES

Woo hoo, here's a phenomenon
Derived from the cute smartphone
The quickest snap from the latest app
And we get cast in web-stone.

I love these selfie shots, don't you?
Of everybody gurning
With smiles so cute they make you puke
And get your stomach turning.

It makes you wonder why they all
Seem rather to be put off
With one arm stretched while we all retch
And ask why arms are cut off?

Well never mind, there's help in kind
The selfie-stick much stronger
Your camera grows by Heaven knows
How many metres longer?

This wand-like clone that holds your phone
Up, up away and farther
Means you can shoot your whole caboot
Mum, sisters, bros and father.

Great stuff, you say, and that's all true
But think about this, please would you?
If selfies shoot what's right in view
Can't make it up now, could you?

Your grandma pissed, your friends just kissed
Your maiden aunt unconscious
Is this how you want folks to view
Your Facebook page so nauseous?

You think it's cool? Well, be the fool
And post those selfies happily
But when your pals cut off your balls
Think on a bit more practically.

Selfies are just great at times
Because they grab good moments
But are they just too full of lust?
Use them to foil opponents.

SYLLABLES

English nouns have come from rounds
Of multi-cultural history
Their forms and shape have us agape
And wondering at their mystery.

But here in Britain's tiddly isles
We prune our nouns like roses
Chop syllables back like smelly cack
So words are bang on noses.

However just across the Pond
(South of the Canadian border)
We bump into the Yankee crew
Whose view is of different order.

Why do these Yanks get into wanks
By adding multi syllables
To nouns just fine as they were defined
And used for years by principals?

Oh no, we've got to take such nouns
And make them into noun-nouns
With extra suffixes so smart
So they don't count as put-downs.

Like conversate, to name just one
I've written on extensively
Whatever happened to 'converse'
Or was it short offensively?

Then who was it who mixed expire
Did it expire too early
For English speakers to catch up
With its next hurly burley?

Well sure as hell, expire was well
Inadequate for Yankees
It's now become the thumping bum
We know as expiration.

These words I take the piss out of
(Apols for the crappy grammar)
I have to say, create dismay
As subtle as a hammer.

OK, we have to move nouns on
In line with evolutions
But save our sanity, please oh please
With sensible solutions.

ICONIC

So many things in today's world
Plain average, not bionic
Just get your face in a public place
And you're instantly iconic.

If you puke and pee very publicly
And deliver that as a comic
You're instantly viewed as somewhat lewd
And right away, iconic.

Just tell some jokes about rich folks
And share some thoughts sardonic
Hey presto! You're no longer crap
In fact, you're now iconic.

Sing a song that hits a few bright wits
And gets some grunts melodic
Online, in muck, who gives a f**k
You're instantly iconic.

Paint a picture full of worms
And say it's ergonomic
Hang it in state at the London Tate
And bingo! You're iconic.

Write a book that takes a look
At sewage tech bionic
You may be it in high tech shit
But also now, iconic.

Got some thoughts on family faults?
Must be socio-economic
As long as it slags those upper-class wags
No worries. You're iconic.

And say you're gay and that's OK?
Of course it is. Harmonic.
But say some stuff that's really rough
And boom. You are iconic.

Now how about the gender shouts
Non-binary sounds exotic!
Just talk about things thereabouts
And you'll soon be iconic.

Let's not forget our own diet
And everything gastronomic
Just say you cook exotic muck
And wow! You'll be iconic.

So what works for all us jerks?
To give us help hedonic?
Forget your brain, just say the inane
And you're sure to become iconic…

AWESOME

'Awesome' is another word
Whose current elevation
To mean 'good' however it should
Is beyond all wild fixation.

Why the f**k should a small truck
Powered by a battery
Be known as 'awesome' just because
Its designer bought some flattery?

How can we all be 'in awe'
Of someone's mediocrity?
Saying 'gosh you're awesome' when in fact
They're just another wannabee?

Can you see why such a word
Is trampled on, so nullified?
'Awesome' was once a good watchword
For brilliant stuff, all bona fide.

Don't know about you, but I stay true
To words like *awesome*'s meaning
Yes, yes, don't gloat: I'm being an old goat
But come on. This is demeaning!

'Awesome' is as awesome does
And I for one want fame for it
Let's find another word for shit
That doesn't deserve a bit of it.

LET'S CONVERSATE

Conversation is an art
That brainy people follow
But brainy types need far more hypes
To make them feel less shallow.

Merely speaking to your friends
Is not enough to please them
(I mean the snots whose kudos rots
When short words don't appease them.)

So what do folks with snob complexes
Do when language fails them?
They simply grab or even nab
More syllables to nail them.

Like why converse, when conversate
Says just the same, but longer?
And no one knows what the hell that goes
For meaning – so it's stronger.

Conversating, after all
Is really more point-scoring
Than simply talking – much like walking
Pedestrian, and boring.

So let's get conversating all
And add that extra syllable
Leap the fence of common sense
And impress those much more gullible.

HOW TO WRITE BETTER

Grammar fascists please take note now
Better not play games with me
Split infinitives then gloat how
You have got away scot-free…

Nor will stupid, foolish use of
Apostrophes in the wrong place
Get you more than my own tough love
(More likely a hard slap-ped face).

Know the difference between 'lose'
And 'loose'? Congratulations.
If I catch you mixing up those
You're forever on short rations.

And while 'you're' thinking of such bores
You'd better pay attention
It's that for 'you are', 'your' is yours
Get it wrong? You're in detention.

'It' is yet another groaner
Fights with 's' time and again
'Its' belongs to its own owner
'It's' … it IS. You got that plain?

Here's a joke, though. You'll enjoy it
Affect's a verb, *effect*'s a noun
Grammar fascists seldom get it
'Effect' can be a verb too, clown…

Now let's see what 'would of happened'
Were that grammatically correct…
'Would HAVE happened' is the right end
Shame on you for grammar wrecked.

Is it 'wrote', or is it 'written'?
Past particles, past tense – what's right?
Trust me, 'I have wrote''s forbidden
FFS get those two things 'write'.

And here's a silly thing (not really)
Can the 'breaks' just stop your car?
Get your spelling right, ideally
'Brakes' will save you from afar.

Writing better isn't about
Being snotty and superior
It's about helping you move out
From being, in a word, inferior.

SMUG

Putting on weight?
Pants getting tighter?
The waist getting far too snug?
Go on a diet and make yourself lighter
Eat clean, eat smart and be Smug.

Driving a car?
A big motor cycle?
Smelly, polluting old slug?
Dump the fuel pumpers and buy a bicycle
Pedal power, pedal pure and be Smug.

Smoke cigarettes?
Like a drink? Puff weed?
Depend on an old-fashioned drug?
Get yourself clean, get away from that need
Substance free, bored to tears, but hey, Smug.

Like to eat meat?
Bacon butties? Rare steak?
Feasting on flesh like a mug?
Now, for your buggered-up arteries' sake
Go veggie – go vegan – be Smug.

Feeling stressed out?
Pissed off? Don't know how?
Brain in a bit of a fug?
Live in the moment: learn mindfulness
Be boringly mindful – but Smug.

Fed up with suburbia?
Hate city dirt?
Feel that some trees need a hug?
Get into glamping - purchase a yurt
Take your clothes off, relax and be Smug.

Got a lump somewhere?
Cancer maybe?
A niggling pain or a bug?
Forget about chemo or old therapy
Take snake oil, fresh air and be Smug.

Stiff in the shoulders?
Sore in your bones?
Just want to lie on the rug?
Start saying 'ohmmmm' and get into the zones
Take up yoga – Namaste – be Smug.

Think you are out there?
Want to be cool?
Then don't be an untrendy mug
Quit all the good stuff that still makes you drool
Be a martyr – be frugal – but Smug.

YUMMY

There is a word that makes me cringe
And feel I want to vommy
I know I really shouldn't whinge
But that damned word is 'yummy'.

It's OK to anthropomorphise
Or baby-speak like Mommy
Or use the F-word some despise
As long as it's not 'yummy'.

Most parents love to hide away
Life's more unpleasant bummies
By using euphemisms, say
But not those f**king 'yummies'.

If Mary Poppins couldn't make
Some sugar fool taste buddies
Then sure as hell we'll never fake
Those medicines, saying they're 'yummies'.

And then we get the yeee-hah folks
Whose speech is less than dummy
Despite being adults fond of jokes
They seriously say 'yummy'.

What do they mean with this foul word
Reminiscent of corpse gummy?
Not its likeness to a turd?
Would that be something 'yummy?'

Even more of nauseous natures
Is the use of this sad termie
When employed by social creatures
Seeking fame being 'yummy'.

Oh, look at my new plastic tuck
A surgical new tummy
Not that you give a flying f**k
But still you call it 'yummy'.

To piss me off you simply use
The word that makes me chuckie
I will always blow a fuse
At nauseating 'yummy'.

WILLY WAVING

Billy is a willy waver
Arrogant – so spoilt and vain
Shouting arguments and bullshit
When his ego's hurt again.

Business meeting, woman speaking
Billy shouts her down of course
Billy's willy gets right knotted
Can't have women showing force!

Next our Billy takes a wander
In his peer group on LinkedIn
Finds some innocent responder
Lands a witty smack on chin.

Metaphorically speaking
Billy's hit the smart bitch right
Making her look foolish although
Billy's facts were not, er, quite…

Smart bitch comes back with a whammy
Makes our Billy look a dick
Billy flees back to his man cave
Hiding his own politic.

Poor old Billy. What a wanker.
Works at his gym day and on
Trying so very hard to conquer
All with just his small hard-on.

Now in case we women
Run into our Billy's shit
What do we do when he's ranting
Say f**k off, or smile a bit?

Billy, like so many guys here
Get your head out of your ass
Use your willy for its purpose
Not for insults, tourist class.

Much as it's hard to grasp how
Willies' actions aren't too smart
Keep yours inside your pants now
Or we'll simply blow a fart.

21ST CENTURY SWEARING

Considering it's rude to swear
We need to think beyond the bend
And come up with new words to bear
That sound OK, but don't offend.

Well, truly I don't give a fluck
It's just a load of trollocks
(That's three, not two, and not so yuk
As the simple pair called bollocks).

How about that dear old crossword clue
Four letters, female, ends UNT
And when you write the C-word you
Get shamed and blamed by your own AUNTie?

Next comes the insipid smell
Of meek, mild words so parodied
Like 'darn' for 'damn' and 'heck' for 'hell'
And other stuff the prudes decreed.

Now think about those things ordure
Like shit and crap, doo-doo, etcetera
And other bashful terms obscure
Can no one think of something betterer?

And then we turn to yellow streams
Like piss and pee and slash so stirred
Why should we go to such extremes
When wee-wee says it in a word?

But chats like this bring us away
From four letters called the F-word
It's something ladies shouldn't say
And men use as a catchword.

No need to feel so thunderstruck
Alternatives are simple tricks
Fluck, Pruck, Shuck, Gruck - even Bruck
Sound good without the politics.

So now it's time for me to swear
Take a scrit, a pree, and swear some more
As the clock does chime I'm quite aware
It's f**k-off time for Suze St Maur.

INTERNATIONAL SWEARING

As you now know, I love to swear
But not only in English
When travelling it helps to curse
In French, in Greek, in Spanish…

Now as for crap and such claptrap
Our choice is wide and beckoning
By using other languages
We can open up the reckoning.

The French word *'merde'* is often aired
In circles philosophical
French folks prefer to use as jokes
This term so scatological.

When Frenchies really want to swear
They tend to go religious
The truly worst French type of curse
Makes God look unprodigious.

Hence *'non de Dieu'* as a fouled-mouth bleurgh
Is worse than shit of all kinds
Or *'putein'*, *'connerie'* and more
That offend most women's thought lines.

Italians go for the term, *'stronzo'*
To name someone most horrible
In fact the word means just plain 'turd'
But in Italy, deplorable.

And while we think 'scatology'
It's well worth us remembering
Modern Greek '*scata*' is still, today
Just shit, if we're not censoring.

Yet I just thank our English wank
Show gratitude when swearing
That when we curse, it's the universe
Not just women we're impairing.

GERMANS

They told me Krauts had serious doubts
And little or no sense of humour
So working with a group of them
Would be a car crash boomer.

I met these folks who 'hated jokes'
In London, at our workplace
And sure enough, they looked that tough
To intimidate a coalface.

Smiles were out. Nobody grinned.
They said hello politely
Some just waved and others chinned
A greeting, meant uptightly.

Oh how could I see eye-to-eye
With people so mysterious?
So many jerks, yet a need to work
With words and pics harmonious?

Our first day dawned with thoughts prolonged
To write in lingos double
How could we write without a fright
Or harsh linguistic trouble?

Well, I wrote words that worked quite well
And their graphics worked superbly
By now, despite the cultural smell
Our output was newsworthy.

And then I learned a lot, lot more
About these German cultures
To start with that these 'quiet' folks
Were southern German vultures.

'Come out with us this Friday night,'
Asked one of my schtum colleagues
'We use the German Wine Bar so
You'll taste our newest follies.'

So off I went one Friday night
And laughed more than I'm able
With Germans whom I thought so tight
But made me fall unable…

Well, no more am I in touch
With 'Germans don't do humour'
I've never laughed so truly much
At these folks' po-faced boomers.

Maybe I've been guided wrongly
Or mistold, of stories old
But for me you Germans strongly
Make me laugh – and that's pure gold.

TWERKING

I wish I had an ass so fit
That I could twerk and jiggle it
Without so much as a slight moan
About its strange desire to roam.

Trouble is my ass is huge
To humourists, a bawdy stooge
So making twerks is not so much
An exercise as pain, as such.

Why I so envy furry beasts
Is, in short, their arsey feats
And what this knowledge should reveal?
The fact that twerks contain a tail.

Back in those millennia
When we were blobs of bleurghia
Crawling out from the oceans' trail
We were all blessed with a tail.

OK, those were Darwin's notions
But unless you hate such motions
Apes and other types were twerking
Long before pop stars were working.

Now, wouldn't twerkers get a blast
From twerking with a longer ass?
A tail to keep that rhythm going
With no risk of tempo slowing?

Evolution here we come now
You robbed us of tails, hum, hum, hum
But since twerking's now on stream
You'd better give tails more esteem.

Who's for growing tails – a pundit?
I for one would gladly fund it
Given my enormous, fat ass
I think fat bums are just first class.

As for things as tough as twerking
My old ass has finished jerking
Fat? OK, but think bum diet
Twerk-free bums are nice and quiet.

'CAN YOU HEAR ME?'

What would we do without our phones
Clamped firmly to our earholes
To share our thoughts most innermost
From here to outer earth poles.

'I'm on the train,' says Ms Pea Brain
'I'll be there in two hours
'And we can chat for all of that
'So let's make that time ours.'

'Yak, yak, yak, yak,' goes Ms Foghorn
With laughter, yelps and guffaws
While sharing her most boring day
And crap about her in-laws.

'Oh please, oh please,' we all cry out
When the train goes through a bad patch
That Madam Foghorn's guttural shout
Gets drowned by a small tech hitch.

Now let's suppose as this thing goes
We're crossing England's Channel
As soon as we go under sea
She's nixed by Euro Tunnel.

For 30 minutes oh, so still
No raucous chat or laughter
Just tea in a cup while she shuts up
And silence rules thereafter.

But not long after, Calais looms
And Foghorn begins booming
No sooner has the train emerged
From sub-aqua unassuming.

This time it's not a lingual clone
Because we're here in France
Right now she's yelling down her phone
'*Suis arrivée!*' Bonne chance…

BODY BUILDING

Pumpy, pumpy, pumpy pump
Body building's such a hump
Grow your muscles giant size
Let your ego aggrandise.

Work your heart out every day
Exercise in every way
Lift those weights until you cry
Worth it to intensify.

Don't forget to check each mirror
Check you're still a training hero
Check how you look in windows too
After all, it's the all-time you.

Now, of course you're supplementing
Gobbling stuff for reinventing
That shit body you were hating
What a major undertaking!

Were you just a skinny wanker
After whom no one would hanker
Silly little specimen
Who needs a shot of creatine?

Let's get going with more such garbage
Swallow down more chemical carnage
Sprinkled with some androgens
Hopefully free from pathogens.

Pumpy, pumpy, pumpy pump
Body building takes a jump
Now you're taking supplements
You're no longer on the fence.

No, it's big time at the gym
You're the main guy – forget him
Need more help? Just on your own?
Try a shot of growth hormone.

Now beyond those painful crunches
Drugs and supplements in bunches
Help you work in your own home
Really get you in the zone.

But there's more, if you're a convert
To this crazy, trendy, jerk art
Glucosamine and chromium
So many supplements – yum, yum

And more too: are you a-quiver?
Trying chewing desiccated liver
Or another well-safe bet
Like purest deer antler velvet?

Course if you're a girlie girl
And think you need to give a whirl
To body building, understand
You'll end up looking like a man.

You'll be like Arnie from the rear
And your tits will disappear
So think twice if that's your pleasure
And contemplate some other leisure.

Pumpy, pumpy, pumpy jump
Are you feeling like a lump?
Body building? Just a whim?
No, let's get back to the gym.

Well, at least the gym's the least thing
That will influence your thinking
Once your mind is into phasing
That great body you've been craving.

Sad, though. As the gym's the right place
Both to work and get some head space
Do yourself a favour, won't you
Avoid the poisons that will tempt you.

Anabolic steroids maybe
Amphetamines to wakey-wakey
Growth hormones and damages
Like Aromatase and androgens.

Still want to build your body out?
Get real, kid. It's a bad shout.
Build your body naturally
And live to old age peacefully.

Politics & Media

OLD BRITANNIA

To be sung to the tune of 'Old MacDonald Had a Farm'. Inspired by the 2016 referendum in Britain on whether or not to leave the European Union.

Old Britannia's in a stew
E-U-E-U-O
First they've got the Brexit crew
E-U-E-U-O
With a leave leave here
And a heave heave there
Here a leave, there a heave
Staying in is naïve
Don't know what the hell to do
E-U-E-U-O

Old Britannia's in a bind
E-U-E-U-O
Remain campaign is well entwined
E-U-E-U-O
With a stay stay here
And a pay pay there
Here a stay, there a pay
Leaving is the twats' way
You must think we're f**king blind
E-U-E-U-O

Old Britannia's got a hitch
E-U-E-U-O
Boris Johnson makes us itch
E-U-E-U-O
With a shout shout here
And a clout clout there
Here a shout, there a clout

So much crap to crank out
Easy when you're bloody rich
E-U-E-U-O

Old Britannia's got some grief
E-U-E-U-O
David Cameron's firm belief
E-U-E-U-O
With a really really here
And a clearly clearly there
Here a really, there a clearly
Shame it's not sincerely
Listen hard, 'cause he's the chief
E-U-E-U-O

Old Britannia's got some pain
E-U-E-U-O
Just what have the Brits to gain
E-U-E-U-O
With some cash cash here
And more tax tax there
Here some cash, there more tax
Or an anti-climax
Britain will be just the same
E-U-E-U-O

ALTERNATIVE FACTS
(Dedicated to the fantasy of USA politics in 2017)

Don't you just love these alternative facts?
Perfect solution to boring truth telling
Simply lie through your teeth with bloody hard whacks
And poof! It's fake news that you're selling.

Now for a change let's create happy facts
So there's no longer cause for a hard grouse
Like, there's been a balls-up: we can all now relax
Homer Simpson's in charge at the White House.

Global warming was next on our list of attack
But we cooled ourselves down again neatly
Shutting up politicians made the temperature slack
No more hot air? No problem. That sweetly.

Next Mr Putin was high on our hacks
But we gave him the chance for a remedy
With a pretty young mare and an outfit Cossacks
They lived ever after so happily.

Scientists finally brought new things to light
About just what foodstuffs are now correct
Turns out all that healthy stuff's simply pure shite
And a McDonald's a day is just perfect.

Political correctness was shaken up silly
When Parliament voted to dump it
Now a spade is a spade, and a willy, a willy
And the word's 'f**k' when anyone humps it.

The F-word, the C-word, they're making comebacks
In schools, in the workplace, in synagogues
No longer obscene but representing 'real' facts
And used freely by Royals and demigods.

So what else can we do with alternative facts?
The prospects for mischief are mind-blowing
We'll nix all the weirdos and other prize twats
And the people who're farting and bellowing.

What a lovely new world we can make for ourselves
Full of fantasy, fun and such happiness
With alternative facts stacked up like bookshelves
Full of beautiful bullshit and crappiness.

One thing that's scary with alternative facts
Although here we can have bits of fun with some
Out there in the real world they're used like an axe
And some silly buggers believe in them...

IN THE HUFF POST
(Should be sung, really)

You'll never guess what I read just today
A recipe for turd pot roast
And it must be so 'cause it's there on show
In the ever truthful Huff Post.

Then I read the next US president
Used to be a TV porn show host
And it must be so 'cause it's there on show
In the ever truthful Huff Post.

Hey girls it's great to masturbate
Tell your friends: go make a proud boast!
And it must be so 'cause it's there on show
In the ever truthful Huff Post.

CHORUS
Hey Arianna, you're just great
Your Huff Post leads society
It gives all of us a real boilerplate
Of respectable impropriety.

Did you know what's in a banana skin?
Shines your shoes and makes good compost
And it must be so 'cause it's there on show
In the ever truthful Huff Post.

Now take a look at your partner's beard
It's a perfect microbe subhost
And it must be so 'cause it's there on show
In the ever truthful Huff Post.

Keep up with the latest penis news
Plus other sexual signposts
And it must be so 'cause it's there on show
In the ever truthful Huff Post.

CHORUS
Hey Arianna, you're just great
Your Huff Post leads society
It gives all of us a real boilerplate
Of respectable impropriety.

Learn how a man fell in love with a goat
Sought a legal marriage on the West Coast
And it must be so 'cause it's there on show
In the ever truthful Huff Post.

Then there's two-headed 10-metre snake
Whose tale shocked all the Ivory Coast
And it must be so 'cause it's there on show
In the ever truthful Huff Post.

Much as I lap up this frivolous crap
Can't believe it, though I do try my utmost
I don't think it's so just because it's on show
In the ever questionable Huff Post.

CHORUS
Hey Arianna, you were great
Your Huffington Post led society
But you sold out to protect your fate
Shame you lost your street credibility.

ABSOLUTELY CLEAR

'Let me make this absolutely clear,'
Say the politicians here
British types just love these words
Largely because they're worthless turds
Of meaningless vocabulary
Standing for f**k all, essentially.

Why should 'clear' now stand for diddly
And give speakers chances piddly
To speak bullshit loud and noisy
So they escape just nice and cosy
From saying what might really show
…the truth? Because they just don't know.

That's why being 'clear' is leery
A warning to expect crap bleary
No sooner do you hear that 'clear' word
Do you think of a well-polished turd…
…which actually means so precious little
You should lose it with your spittle?

So what other words could these guys
Use as more powerful verbal allies
To convince us that they're knowing
More than what their bullshit's showing?
Words that we can count on, maybe?
Truths that resonate – hey, baby…

Nah. It's 'absolutely clear' to think that
Politicians just don't know what
Is the difference in between
Their asshole and a wolverine
Let's make this absolutely clear
Politics really is small beer.

That's a shame when you consider
These twats have power – I do not kidder!
So, politicos, grow up and make
Strides to stop this awful pisstake
Tell us where it's really at
D'you think you might just manage that?

Oh, maybe not, if so I'm sorry
Wouldn't want to cause you worry
Especially when you work so hard
To make yourselves so plainly heard
It's 'absolutely clear', M'Lud
Your politics are as clear as mud.

'YANKEE DOODLE' RE-WRITTEN

To be sung to the tune of 'Yankee Doodle Dandy'. Written in honour of the US Independence Day, July 4th.

Yankee Doodle drank some tea
Straight from Boston harbour
Damn those Brits, gave him the shits
So Yankee couldn't ride far.

CHORUS:
Yankee Doodle keep it right
Yankee Doodle zappy
Mind your manners day and night
And let the West be happy.

Dad and I flew overseas
To Europe bright and breezy
But what we found right on the ground
Was not what you'd call easy.

Chorus

People made us welcome, sure
Europe loves a Yankee
But when politics occur
They think we're pretty wankee.

Chorus

Now that British tea had made
All the Yankees poop more
Gave the Yankees great ideas
For worldwide faster food power.

Chorus

Fortunately Uncle Sam
Has travelled far and yonder
Yankee food hits just the mood
Wherever humans wander.

Chorus

Politics and other tricks
Just get forgotten chop, chop
When British fans make dinner plans
At the old fish and chip shop.

Chorus

What's to eat is such a treat
Makes politics look boring
Now Yankee Doodle food is here
Even the Queen's adoring…

Chorus

And so the Brits and Yanks do well
To stuff their greedy faces
Politics can go to hell
While fries and burgers please us.

Chorus

Yankee Doodle crossed the sea
Though Boston tea still labours
But Happy Independence Day
You lovely US neighbours!

REALITY TV

Dontchya love reality
When it's expressed on your TV?
Nothing like folks' dirty clothes
And stinky socks or filthy hose…
…to make you laugh and smile and puke
And giggle, snort without rebuke
All safely shut away inside
Your television's plastic hide.

Watch those stars eat bugs and snakes
Stuffing down what nature makes…
…most putrid and disgusting, plus
They lose if they should make a fuss.
Hey, why should people getting paid
A good few grand for having stayed
In a jungle camping ground
Bitch and moan and piss around?

And if your taste is not in favour
Of revolting food to savour
There is much more real TV
To choose from internationally.
For example, baking cakes
Or cooking meals from emu steaks
Or making someone's backyard fly
From shitehole to mini Versailles.

If you're not domestic, that's
No problem. Just change habitats.
Check the shagging, moans and groans
Of contestants paying off loans
By writhing nude on sandy shores

And bonking really awful bores
All in the name of pure romance
True love blooms well, without its pants.

And if you like real tits and butts
The size of largish garden huts
With robberies and wild hysterics
Nervous breakdowns, frantic antics
Cleavages, bum cracks and all
…that make the Grand Canyon look small
You need look no further than
The nearest kool Kardashian.

Frankly, though, what's entertaining
Most of all, without restraining
What you can believe or not
Is on the news your country's got
All you need to watch on full
Is politicians' load of bull
Such stupid crap from brainless yuppies
You really couldn't make it uppies.

POTUS AND FLOTUS

POTUS and FLOTUS in Twenty Seventeen
A mismatch-ed couple, now that is for sure
Age, sex and customs of distance extreme
And lack of each other's original culture.

One thing in common though, easy to spot
So simple to see why they congregated
Brain cells that simply don't function a lot
And IQs that seem really 'bigly' stagnated.

POTUS now is on wife number three-ish
They get much younger as he yet gets older
But this one's reluctance to be cosy-up-ish
Makes my regard for her bolder and bolder.

People say that dear FLOTUS was in it for bucks
And OK, that may be true or may be not
But having to smile through what obviously sucks?
That is more than her pre-reckoned work lot.

FLOTUS avoids him when it's time to hold hands
As has been seen several times in the media
Can you blame lovely FLOTUS ignoring his plans
When you think where his hands have been gropin' ya?

'Grab by the pussy,' POTUS once spoke of women
Makes you wonder just when this was referring to
Was it way before FLOTUS became his prize brood hen
Or was it since, when POTUS was married to?

And then we see manners – or sheer lack thereof
With POTUS striding up, down on various aircraft
Poor FLOTUS struts behind, also ran, so unloved
While he saves his hair from the wind and downdraft.

Now here's a new talent that POTUS has hon-ed
Shoving other world leaders aside out of our sight
The Montenegro Head Honcho was quickly dethrone-ed
When our POTUS pushed past him and stole his key limelight.

One thing that makes me smile over and over
Is what Vladimir must find highly amusing
No wonder he thinks dear POTUS is a pushover
With such public behaviour so dumb and abusing.

POTUS, stop treating young FLOTUS so badly
It's worse for your image than those Mexican walls
Suggests that you're nothing more, so very sadly,
Than a big mouth with small brain and no proper balls.

BIGLY

What a f**king stupid word
Shared by that POTUS prize nerd
Bigly. Bugly. So absurd.

Why should we just now submit
To English that's archaic shit
When all it's doing is coining spit?

Much as politicians shout
Rant and thunder all about
Shit like this? It has no clout.

So, what's in word you ask?
'Specially when said by an ass?
Simple: media's big class.

Take up a word that no one's heard
Since Shakespeare used that short adverb
Who's he trying to kid, that turd?

Now we're stuck with nonsense word
Hitting headlines read and heard
Taking us back to the average nerd.

One thing seems more than a whim
Is that dickhead's synonym
A perfect term to suit just him?

Bigly? I don't think so now.
'Cos bigly doesn't show us how
To see beyond this puppet show.

There's no point polishing a turd
So let's forget this bugly word
And to its creator, flip the bird.

Seasonal

DRY CHRISTMAS

Dedicated to the victims of the UK's Cumbria floods in 2015 and all subsequent heavily rainy episodes – and we get a lot. To be sung to the tune of 'I'm Dreaming of a White Christmas'

I'm dreaming of a dry Christmas
Just like that day back in July
When the sun was out for
A half-hour or more
And all my laundry load got dry.

I'm dreaming of a dry Christmas
With every raindrop here that falls
May the sleet not drip down my walls
And may the plumber please be on call.

I'm dreaming of a dry Christmas
When all my bedding is not damp
When I don't go mopping
The floor after shopping
And don't get rain-related cramp.

I'm dreaming of a dry Christmas
Without those sandbags at the door
May the rain not spread 'cross the floor
And may booze be the only thing to pour.

DONALD THE POLITICIAN

Written for Christmas 2016 in the light of 2016's USA election. To be sung to the tune of 'Rudolph the Red-Nosed Reindeer'.

Donald, the politician
Has a very bad toupé
Billowing from his forehead
Coloured just like dried-out hay.

All of the paparazzi
Laugh at him and call him names
Even his own staff members
Long to see his hair in flames.

Then one wet election day
Barack comes to say
'Donald, with your hair so lush,
We are going to kick your tush.'

Then all the voters giggle
When they see dear Hillary
Grab Donald's fluffy toupé
Trumping his whole comedy.

Suddenly he's just an egg-head
Like a shiny billiard ball
Just like that poor old Samson
When Delilah shaved his skull.

Now that Donald's got no hair
US folks can say
That's just one of his pitfalls
Does he also have no balls?

Donald, the politician
Have a happy Christmas time
Make sure you get some new hair
Ready for your future slime.

POST CHRISTMAS POEM

Christmas is over
The turkey is gone
Dismembered, digested
And perfectly spun…

…into many waste products
Down sewers and wells
In unmentionable forms
With unmentionable smells.

We who have cooked this
Are weary and tired
It's like running a restaurant
Wrongly acquired.

If anyone asks me
For more bits of turkey
I'll smack 'em so hard
Their faces won't worky.

Cranberry sauce?
More gravy and stuffing?
Go fix it yourselves
And no, I'm not bluffing.

My nails are all broken
My makeup is running
To think before Christmas
I looked pretty stunning.

Now I resemble
A butcher in manners
With meat smells and fingers
That look like bananas.

My stomach is bulging
My hair is all matted
My face looks a bit like
A ball that's been batted.

My clothes are all splattered
With goose grease and gravy
And water stains just like
You'd get in the navy.

So what am I going to
Cook for tomorrow?
Roast beef? Roast chicken?
A nifty stuffed marrow?

A roast pork with crackling?
A juicy roast duck?
Now, here's the bad news
I don't give a f**k.

My time of delivering
These tasty creations
Has come to an end
I've just made reservations…

…for a restaurant, (risking
Being slightly offensive)
As I love their food
But it's f**king expensive.

And here's the bonus
Oh, love of my life
You're paying for the whole meal
To honour your wife.

'JINGLE BILLS'
To be sung to the tune of 'Jingle Bells'

Oh, Jingle Bills, Jingle Bills
Christmas makes us pay
Oh, what utter hell it is
When New Year comes to stay.

Oh, Jingle Bills, Jingle Bills
Coming through the door
Piling up brown envelopes
A-gathering on the floor.

Crashing through the year
On credit and on fear
O'er the top we go
When Christmas time is near.

Bills materialise
Scaring us away
What hell it is to realise
We've 30 days to pay.

Oh, Jingle Bills, Jingle Bills
January sucks
Oh, what have we done to spend
So many precious bucks.

Jingle Bills, Jingle Bills
Spending much decreased
No more fancy food or booze
Till Easter time at least.

DAFFODILS? IN JANUARY?
(*A tribute to William Wordsworth, and a true story*)

I wandered lonely, cursing loud
At mud and shit o'er vales and hills
When all at once I clasped my brow
F**k me, those must be daffodils
In January? What a wheeze
This global warming's the bee's knees.

Continuous for several feet
This row of daffs was here to stay
Not puny buds but real blooms, neat
And in a balls-out upright way
They took me in at a simple glance
While I drove by, by sheer pure chance.

The road beside them heaved with mud
Splashed my whole car with watery pee
And other quite unmentionable crud
Such inappropriate crap to see
I gazed – and gazed – and then, a hitch
My car was aiming for the ditch.

Today, when on my couch I lay
Recuperating here of course
I still see all those daffs that day
And think about the powerful force
When, distracted, I did wedge
My car into the neighbour's hedge.

FIREWORKS NIGHT

Guy Fawkes, I want a word with you
You bumbling, clumsy nitwit
The fact you failed what the Plot entailed
Has left us really paying for it.

Had you got blowing Parliament up
Done properly in the first place
We'd not have had to suffer each
November's noisy fart race.

For 400 years and plus by now
We've had to try to put right
Your stupid, crass ineptitude
By setting fire to cordite.

Now if that weren't just bad enough
There's all that crap food fervour
While barbecues and fires burn
Cheap sausages and burgers.

You eat them in the dark of course
In buns or rolls a-blazing
But burn your hands on one end
While the other end is freezing.

And soon the lovely little Tommy
Steps in dog shit in the gloom
Tracks it into your Mercedes
Leaving everlasting fumes.

Then young Millie grasps a sparkler
By the wrong end when aflame
Screams with fright and pain, poor Millie
Off you go to the Emergency Room.

When eventually you get back home
Wondering why your shed's a-glow
You realise your neighbour's fireworks
Turned it into a bonfire show.

As I said, my dear old Guy Fawkes
You have much to answer for
Had you managed to blow it all up
At least this shite we could ignore.

VALENTINE'S DAY

(*The following inspired by Browning's beautiful words…*)

On Valentine's Day just last year
I slapped my true love round the ear
It came up in a blister
So he slept with my sister
Then left, shouting 'tough titty, dear!'

Oh Valentine, will you be mine?
For your love, I really do pine!
What's that? You would rather
Stick a knife in your father?
Piss off then, you're well out of line.

Let's hear it for Valentine's Day!
Nonstop kisses and hugs and foreplay
It's all hearts and flowers
For 24 hours
Then it's back to our bitch-slapping way.

VALENTINE'S DAY CARD VERSES FROM HELL
(Not all original – some traditional/anonymous ones are included.)

Love may be fabulous, sweetness and bliss,
But I only wed you 'cause I'd been on the piss.

I thought that I could love no other,
Until, that is, I met your brother.

Your eyes were like diamonds picked out to adorn 'yer'
More like baseball diamonds with sacks in each corner.

Of loving beauty you floated with grace
If only you could have hidden your face.

Kind, intelligent, loving and hot,
This describes everything you were not.

You were such a hero when I was in labour
Left me in peace while you slept with our neighbour.

I loved to be with you from when newlywed
As long as you left that paper bag on your head.

I loved your smile, your face, and your eyes –
Such a shame I'm so clever at telling lies.

My sweetheart, my lover, my beautiful wife
Marrying you really screwed up my life.

You were all I could ask for to make a great hubby
So sad you went bald and turned out really chubby.

I saw your face when I was dreaming
That's why I always woke up screaming.

My sweetheart, you took my breath away;
What strange disease made you stink this way?

You were always so active – a lover of all sports
That's why I had to divorce a whole golf course.

My feelings for you no words could tell,
Except for maybe 'go to hell'.

What inspired this loving rhyme?
Two parts tequila, one part lime.

Your face was just perfect, your body divine,
They looked even better with each glass of wine.

Now how should I phrase this romantic epistle?
You resembled a bulldog licking piss off a thistle.

ROSES ARE RED
(Again, not all original – some traditional/anonymous ones are included.)

Roses are red, violets are blue, sugar is sweet, and so are you.
But the roses were fading, the violets were dead, the sugar bowl's empty and so was your head.

Roses are red, violets are blue
Sugar's unhealthy and so are you.

Roses are red, violets are blue
Sorry I'm snotty, but I've got the flu.

Roses are red, violets are blue
Never mind shagging, just pass me a brew.

Roses are red, violets are blue
I'm quite good-looking; what happened to you?

Roses are red, violets are blue
Life was OK until I met you.

Roses are red, violets are blue
Why that should be, I haven't a clue.

Roses are red, violets are blue
Please put the seat down when you've used the loo.

Violets are blue, roses are red
I hate your guts and I wish you were dead.

Violets are blue, roses are red
The last thing I'd go near is your smelly bed.

Violets are blue, roses are red
You don't look too bad with that bag on your head.

Violets are blue, roses are red
Shame your backside is the size of a shed.

Violets are blue, roses are red
Your beard is smelly – why not shave off your head?

VALENTINE'S DAY WITH THE GRAMMAR POLICE

Roses are red, violets are blue
That's just a cliché. Don't like it? Go screw.

Violets is blue, roses is red,
Get noun/verbs together, you puerile dickhead.

And roses are red while violets are blue
Don't start with conjunctions, they're strictly taboo.

I'll love you my dearest to the moon and back
Please don't exaggerate or I'll give you a smack.

Take my heart its yours on a plate
Keep it till you learn how to punctuate.

I think I love you, or maybe its fantasy?
Never mind that. Where's the f**king apostrophe?

To truly love you, that's what I intend
You split an infinitive: you're not my friend.

Posies are cosies and I love your nosies
Please! Shove the poetry - I just love grossies.

Cherie, *je t'aime et j'aimerais te baiser*
French doesn't fool me. You want an 'easy'.

I think I love you my dear Valentine
Get off the pot and decide: are you mine?

Your the one lover I wants to discover
Well, keep on looking. Your grammar's a bummer.

I love your face!!! And your eyes!!! And your glamour!!!
Those exclamation marks need a hit with a hammer.

Since encountering yourself I am thunderstruck
Get over it, dipstick. Those long words just suck.

Sweetheart, you're stunning, a beautiful dame
F**k off and next time try to recall my name.

Your eyes are like diamonds that sparkle in light
That simile's awful. Clichéd and pure shite.

Conversating with you is sweet to my ears
Don't be pretentious. Let's have a few beers.

You are my heavenly gift from the gods
You're why I still need to keep kissing frogs.

EASTER BEASTER

Yummy* Mummy just loves Easter
Rabbits, chicks, cute eggs and stuff
All her friends, too, have increased her
…appetite for schmaltzy puff.

With such foul proliferation
Of this holiday's sheer spin
It's creating consternation
'Cos commercial crooks creep in.

Now it's not enough to hard-boil
…eggs for colouring and dyeing
Nor is it enough for snake oil
To give consumers a good hiding.

No. Today it's just another
Chance for commerce to cash in.
Did you know you now should bother
With Easter decorations for your kin?

Wrap your home up in such cute shit
That your folks will fairly puke
Easter Tree with baubles on it?
What a f**king awful fluke.

Then there's Easter cards to send off
Spend a lot on them and postage
Why should people want to wank off
On a thought so based on wastage?

And don't forget your reservations
At a restaurant so handy
Home-cooked Easter's innovations
Don't do much for the greedy grandee.

Now, how else does Easter cut rough?
Sales of furry eggs and chicks?
Hideously fattening food stuff?
Sold by such uncaring pricks?

If you're Christian, Easter's crucial
If you're not, we still respect it
Flip the bird to shit so brutal
That's not how we should reflect it.

If you're like that Yummy Mummy
And you want those chicks and rabbits
Bear in mind that homes get slummy
When those small creatures get the shits.

How about just being normal
…while in most countries Westernised?
Simply take time off informal
And say f**k off to 'pressurised'.

* Also see 'Yummy' in Chapter Four.

Also available from Corona Books UK

Corona Books is an independent publishing company, newly established in 2015. We aim to publish the brilliant, innovative and quirky, regardless of genre. A selection of our other titles follows on the next pages. All our books are available on Amazon.co.uk and Amazon worldwide.

www.coronabooks.com

Please visit our website for the latest on other and forthcoming titles, and to sign up for our e-newsletter. We promise we won't bombard you with emails and you can unsubscribe at any time.

Frogmorton Culpepper Saves the World

Keith Trezise

A new scientifically fictitious novel that makes *Hitchhiker's Guide to the Galaxy* read like a municipal guide to manhole covers?

Frogmorton Culpepper didn't wake up on the day he got fired expecting to save the world, not that week at least. He had to prove out his environmental technology experiments to his superiors first. The world had yet to provide any recognition of his genius. His mother had yet to provide any recognition of his ability to do anything. The girl of his dreams had yet to provide any recognition of his existence. Some, if not all, of that changes in *Frogmorton Culpepper Saves the World*, a work of the scientifically fictitious that if it doesn't change your life forever, will at least make you smile (a lot) .... and if you want to know why there's a picture of a cleverly-folder origami rhinoceros on the cover, all we can say is that you'll have to read the book.

The Great British Limerick Book

Lewis Williams

Surely it can't be done. But it has been done. For the first time in the history of mankind someone has been dedicated enough and fool enough to write a filthy limerick for every town in the UK which, unlike Leeds or Devizes, doesn't already have a classic filthy limerick to call its own.

From Land's End to John o' Groats, *The Great British Limerick Book* has a filthy limerick for your town, for your uncle's town, for your cousin's husband's ex-wife's town …. as long as it's in the UK and as long as it isn't one of those few places that are really impossible to find a rhyme for.

There are over 900 limericks in the book. A lot of them are hilarious. Most of them are very funny. All of them are filthy.

The Oxbridge Limerick Book

Lewis Williams

Presenting the very finest in vulgar humour, *The Oxbridge Limerick Book* revives the ancient and noble art of the filthy limerick, injects it with a large dose of twenty-first century humour and applies it to the venerable institutions of Oxford and Cambridge, giving every college in the two universities a filthy limerick to call its own. The results will cause hilarity and provoke outrage, with what is quite possibly the best and most original little book of filthy limericks to be published since 1928.

About the author

Lewis Williams went to Darwin College, Cambridge (for one evening, that is, in 2015 for a dinner he was invited to.) On the other hand, he did genuinely work at Oxford University for a number of years. His ignominious departure from its employ had nothing whatsoever to do with his writing rude limericks concerning the place or its employees. He is the author of *The Great British Limerick Book* and *The Scottish Limerick Book*. He hasn't devoted the whole of his recent past to the art of writing filthy limericks, either. He is also up to over level 400 on Candy Crush.

www.ingramcontent.com/pod-product-compliance
Lightning Source LLC
Chambersburg PA
CBHW031446040426
42444CB00007B/1004